Perfect Your Sentences

Peter Howard

 LONGMAN

Longman Australia Pty Limited
Longman House
Kings Gardens
95 Coventry Street
Melbourne 3205 Australia

Offices in Sydney, Brisbane, Adelaide and Perth,
and associated companies throughout the world.

Designed by Sylvia Witte
Illustrated by Randy Glusac
Set in 11/12pt Helvetica Roman
Produced by Longman Australia Pty Ltd
through Longman Malaysia, PA

National Library of Australia
Cataloguing-in-publication data

Howard, Peter.
   Perfect your sentences.

   ISBN 0 582 65947 7

   1. English language — Sentences — Problems, exercises,
   etc. 2. English language — Grammar — Problems,
   exercises, etc. I. Title.

428.2

Foreword

This book has been compiled for the use, at school or at home, of pupils who wish to improve the quality and variety of their sentences.

Rules and guidelines are given, using as little linguistic terminology as possible, followed by practice sentences which should be written in full. All work can be done in a pupil's book, or on paper. Answers are provided so that all sentences can be corrected.

Contents

Topics
Improving — vocabulary
   Exercises 2, 6, 14, 16, 21, 34, 44, 70, 71
Varying — word order
   Exercises 5, 11, 22, 23, 25, 28, 37, 41, 50, 59, 78
Varying — sentence beginnings
   Exercises, 1, 3, 5, 8, 39, 42
Joining or combining
   Exercises 4, 7, 10, 26, 32, 38, 40, 43, 45, 47, 53, 79
Correction — redundant words
   Exercises 27, 55
Correction — faulty sentences
   Exercises 9, 49, 54, 61, 69, 75, 78, 80, 84
Verbs — tense, mood, voice
   Exercises 31, 52, 62, 68, 81
Number
   Exercises 33, 36, 46, 56, 60, 66, 73
Pronouns
   Exercises 26, 29, 32, 79, 82
Nonstandard English
   Exercises 35, 48, 57, 72
Grammar and usage
   Exercises 12, 13, 17, 18, 19, 20, 24, 30, 51, 58, 63, 64, 65,
         67, 74, 76, 77, 83

Exercises

1 Statements into questions

A sentence that tells us something is a **statement**. One way it can be changed into a **question** is to use 'does', 'do' or 'did' as the first word.

Dirk enjoys playing tennis. (*statement*)
Does Dirk enjoy playing tennis? (*question*)

Make question sentences from these statements, using 'does', 'do' or 'did'.

1   Sharon now makes models from clay. (*Change the form of the verb.*)
2   David goes to school by train. (*Change the form of the verb.*)
3   The children practise the violin each morning.
4   Our team played well yesterday. (*Change the form of the verb.*)

2 Overworked words — 'got'

Write each sentence using a word from the box in place of the one in brackets.

acquired   caught   earned   coaxed   became   scored

1   My brother (got) two hundred dollars a week.
2   In the first half, the winger (got) a try.
3   While holidaying in Toronto, Terry (got) a strong Canadian accent.
4   She (got) the cat to eat some of the fish.
5   In the jungle, many of the men (got) sick.
6   Luckily she (got) the last train from Sydney.

3 To emphasise a word, try placing it first

Though he was hurt, he played well.
Hurt though he was, he played well. (*emphasis on the word
'hurt'*)

Rewrite the sentences below, placing the underlined word first.
Read your sentences, and notice how the meaning changes.

1 As she was <u>shocked</u>, she could not find her way.
2 The frightened bird flew <u>up</u>.
3 I would like only his old photograph <u>for</u> myself. (*Use a
   comma.*)
4 The guns boomed out <u>unceasingly</u>.

4 Join these sentences by using 'when'

Use 'when' in the middle for two sentences.
Use 'when' at the beginning for two sentences.

1 The children went to the zoo. They saw a baby koala.
2 We can go to the park. The weather clears.
3 The game finished. Everybody went home.
4 It is dark in this room. The lights are turned off.

5 To vary and improve sentences, you can begin them with adjectives

Rewrite these sentences, beginning with a suitable adjective
from the box.

lumbering   experienced   camouflaged   interesting

1 Torpedo boats were anchored in the tiny cove.
2 Dinosaurs roamed the earth at that time.
3 Players are needed for the tour to England.
4 Books filled the shelves in her study.

6 Repeating words can give extra effect

By repeating a word, extra effect is obtained. Be careful, however, not to do this too often when writing a story.

Complete these sentences, using pairs of words from the box.

<table>
<tr><td>Nearer and nearer   Bang! Bang!   'Help! Help!'
Down, down</td></tr>
</table>

1 . . . . shrieked the frightened child.
2 . . . . came the figure dressed in black.
3 . . . . sank the torpedoed ship.
4 . . . . went the pistol, as he took careful aim.

7 Use 'and' to join similar ideas; use 'but' to join contrasting ideas

Rain began to fall **and** the creek rose rapidly.
It was a sunny day, **but** the wind was bitterly cold. (*Notice that 'but' needs a comma before it*.)

Use 'and' or 'but' to join these sentences.

1 The police arrived first. The ambulance came soon after.
2 Their front door was open. Nobody was at home.
3 His rope was thin. It was very strong.
4 Donald took out his pen. He began to make notes. (*Leave out 'He'*.)

8 One way to vary and improve sentences is to begin them with adverbs

Adverbs sometimes need a comma after them. In two of these sentences, the adverb needs to be separated from the other words by a comma.

1   The tennis matches will start tomorow.
2   The strong wind howled outside.
3   Koalas grunt sometimes.
4   Paul rushed wildly into the room.

9   Correcting mistakes

Rewrite these sentences, changing the form of the underlined verb, which is incorrect.

1   We all <u>swum</u> at the beach yesterday.
2   Have you <u>wrote</u> to thank your aunt?
3   William <u>drunk</u> all the ginger beer.
4   The bell for school has already <u>rang</u>.
5   The cow has <u>trod</u> on my sweet peas.
6   Her new shorts <u>shrunk</u> after a week.

10   Two simple sentences can be made into one by using describing words from the second sentence

The plane was climbing quickly. The plane was powerful.
The **powerful** plane was climbing quickly.

A boar charged the hunter. It was extremely savage.
An **extremely savage** boar charged the hunter.

Join each pair of sentences below, using describing words in this way.

1   The soldiers attacked at dawn. The soldiers were brave.
2   Several dogs came close. They were wild.
3   The wind sprang up suddenly. It was very strong.
4   The sun beat down on the horsemen. It was painfully hot.

11   Three ways of writing a sentence

The boy will probably win, because he has trained hard.
The boy, who has trained hard, will probably win.
The winner will probably be the boy who has trained hard.

Rewrite the sentences below. Each is modelled on one of those above. Write two more sentences, using the other pattern. (Write four sentences altogether.)

1   Susan, who is making many mistakes, will probably lose.
2   One pupil will probably be a painter, because she is very gifted.

12   'Can' and 'may'

'Can' denotes ability to do something. 'May' asks permission.

Write each sentence below, using the correct word from the brackets.

1   (Can May) I go to the pictures after lunch, Mother?
2   (Can May) you come here and hold the ladder?
3   (Can May) I come in?

13   Avoid double negatives

Never use a negative verb and a negative qualifier together.
Correct these sentences by altering the underlined words.

1   He <u>hasn't</u> nothing to declare at the airport.
2   Megan <u>can't</u> hardly wait until her birthday.
3   There <u>wasn't</u> nobody at the front door.
4   They <u>hadn't</u> scarcely enough feed for their cattle.

14 Phrases add meaning to verbs

Improve these sentences by adding an adjectival phrase.
Choose your answers from the phrases in the box.

of hoodlums	on the mountain	in the river
	in a black coat	

1   The crocodiles snapped angrily at the boat.
2   A man suddenly appeared.
3   A gang stood in front of my brother.
4   The castle was heavily bombed during the war.

15 Completing sentences from the text

Four pupils from our school entered the local swimming
carnival. Unfortunately, Stephanie did not progress beyond her
heats. Judith came fourth in the 200 metres freestyle final.
Arnold won the 100 metres backstroke easily. Terry was
unlucky to come second, by a touch, in the 1500 metres.

Complete the four sentences below, using information given in
the text. Begin each sentence with the words in bold type.

1   Write what **four pupils from our school** did.
2   Write the name of **one person who never reached the
    finals**.
3   Write where **Judith came**, and in which race.
4   Write by whom **the 100 metres backstroke was won**.

16 Phrases add meaning to verbs

Improve your sentences by adding an adverbial phrase. Choose your answers from the phrases in the box.

> in the breeze   with some pliers   to every house
> by the waves

1 She carefully unscrewed the lid.
2 Houses near the beach were damaged.
3 Flags of many nations waved proudly.
4 The boys on bicycles delivered pamphlets.

17 'Less' and 'fewer'

'Less' refers to a quantity that cannot be counted. 'Fewer' refers to a number that can be counted.

I am eating **less butter**. We caught **fewer fish**.

Write the sentences below, choosing the correct word from the brackets.

1 There were (less fewer) children in the class than expected.
2 We were given (less fewer) work today than yesterday.
3 The use of seat belts in cars has led to (less fewer) fatalities.

18 Adjective or adverb?

Write these sentences, choosing the correct words from those in brackets.

1 The team did not play too (good well) last season.
2 We have not picked (near nearly) enough yet.
3 My grandmother was walking (slow slowly) past.
4 Come to my house as (quick quickly) as possible.
5 We had a (really real) excellent time at the party.
6 Sharon won her race (easily easy).

19 The verbs 'lie' and 'lay' are often confused

To lie means to rest: I lie, I am lying, I was lying, I lay or I have lain on the bed.

To lie also means to not tell the truth: I lie, I am lying, I was lying, I lied or I have lied.

To lay means to put something down (lay an egg, lay the table): I lay, I am laying, I was laying, I laid or I have laid the plate on the table.

Write each sentence, choosing the correct word from those in brackets.

1   Dad has (laid lain) on the sofa all morning.
2   Marjorie says she has already (lain laid) the table.
3   The book was (lain laid) on the chest of drawers.
4   I would like to (lay lie) in the sun this morning.
5   While (laying lying) in bed, I had an idea.
6   Each day she (lays lies) her books neatly on the desk.

20 Using the words 'kind' and 'kinds'

The word 'kind' is singular and should be used with 'this' or 'that' to modify a singular noun. The word 'kinds' is plural and should be used with 'these' or 'those' to modify plural nouns. The same rule applies to other words — 'sort', 'type' and 'class'.

Correct each of these sentences by altering the underlined word.

1   I like these <u>kind</u> of apples.
2   Do you prefer this sort of meat <u>pies</u>?
3   That kind of <u>coffees</u> is sold everywhere.
4   Those are the kinds of <u>day</u> I like.
5   These <u>type</u> of cars are very fast.
6   This class of <u>animals</u> is rare.

21 Overworked words — 'nice'

Write each sentence below, using a word from the box in place of the one in brackets.

handsome   delicious   enjoyable   kind   fragrant   tasteful

1   Mother cooked some pasta which was (nice).
2   In the lounge room were (nice) curtains.
3   He wore some (nice) perfume to the disco.
4   The three days in Fiji were (nice).
5   I think the male vocalist is (nice).
6   My uncle is always (nice) to visitors.

22 Position of the word 'only'

The word 'only' should be written in front of and next to the word or phrase it modifies.

Write each sentence putting in the word 'only' to suit the meaning.

1   David may sleep on the bed. (David and nobody else may use the bed.)
2   David may sleep on the bed. (David may sleep nowhere else.)
3   David may sleep on the bed. (David may sleep on the only bed there is.)
4   David may sleep on the bed. (David may sleep — but do nothing else — upon the bed.)

23 Three ways of writing about the subject

A small, pretty girl stepped from the bus.
A girl, small and pretty, stepped from the bus.
A girl, who was small and pretty, stepped from the bus.

Rewrite, twice, each of the sentences below. Use the second and third constructions given in the examples above.

1   The hungry, exhausted dog lay in the gutter.
2   A sharp, pointed spike had been driven into the ground.

24 Adjective or adverb?

Write these sentences, choosing the correct words from those in brackets.

1   His old car goes (quick quickly), but sounds (noisily noisy).
2   She held the money (tight tightly), even though her arm hurt (bad badly).
3   Did you do (good well) in the test after not feeling (good well)?

25 Different ways of arranging words

Arrange each group of words in four different ways to make four sentences. In each case use only the words given. In some of your sentences you will need to add commas.

1   ship violently the storm rocked the
2   masterpiece artist painstakingly the his worked at

26 Joining with a preposition and 'which'

Join each sentence below with a pair of words from the box:
You will need to add a comma to some of them. Number 6
should be written in two different ways.

for which	to which	from which
on which	with which	in which

1   We bought some lemons. We extracted the juice.
2   Steven lent me a mattress. I slept soundly.
3   I picked up a stick. I killed the snake.
4   There was a towbar on the car. We attached the trailer.
5   My aunt gave me her sewing machine. I was very grateful.
6   The plane was comfortable. We travelled in it.

27 Avoid words that repeat an idea

Look at the groups of words in the box. The underlined word or
words can be left out. They are not necessary.

<u>up</u> until	fall <u>down</u>	<u>free</u> gift	blue <u>in colour</u>
refer <u>back</u>	continue <u>on</u>	followed <u>after</u>	

Rewrite these sentences, which contain repeated ideas.

1   Dad was offered a free gift by the firm.
2   We continued on to the next village.
3   The dog followed after the rabbit into the hole.
4   Her car was here up until this morning.
5   The river was brown in colour after the rains.
6   A plate fell down from the shelf.
7   You will need to refer back to the previous page.

28 Place phrases or clauses so that they relate clearly to the words they modify

Move a phrase or clause in each of these sentences so that they will make sense.

1   We could see many kinds of fish cruising in the glass-bottomed boat.
2   We gave all the scraps to the geese that were ready to throw away.
3   She left the bread on the counter that was too hard to eat.
4   I bought a clock from a dealer with crooked hands.
5   I could see the mountain clearly flying at a thousand feet.
6   I read that the burglar had been caught in the paper.

29 Use the right pronoun

Pronouns that are used as subjects of verbs are:
   I, he, she, we, they, you
Pronouns that are used as objects of verbs or prepositions are:
   me, him, her, us, them, you (Notice that 'you' does not change.)

She is older than **I** ('I' is the subject of the verb 'am', which is understood in this sentence.)
He is my teacher. ('He' is the subject of the verb 'is'.)
I tackled **him**. ('Him' is the object of the verb 'tackled'.)
Terry sat above **me**. ('Me' is the object of the preposition 'above'.)

Write each sentence choosing the correct pronoun from those in brackets.

1   Neither Robert nor (I me) have been to the opera.
2   The farmer offered Susan and (I me) a job.
3   I can swim as fast as (she her).
4   He thinks that (us we) two can win the doubles match.
5   Between you and (I me) there are few secrets.
6   Both (him he) and I are going to the beach.

30 'Bring' and 'take'

'Bring' should be used when something is being moved **towards** the speaker

Bring me that paper.

'Take' should be used when something is being moved **away from** the area of the speaker.

Take that paper with you.
I must take the paper with me.

Rewrite the sentences below, using the correct verbs.

1   I am uncertain what to bring when I leave for Japan.
2   I shall bring my brother with me when I go.
3   Shall I bring her a cup of tea in bed?
4   Take that book to me at my desk.

31 Keep verbs in the same tense

If you begin writing in the past tense, don't change to the present. In the following paragraph, the writer starts in the present, changes to the past and then goes back to the present.

Fifty-five years before Jesus is born, the Romans land in Britain. They fought the Britons and took much of their land. Caradoc was a Briton who would not give in. He is the chief and the Romans called him Caractacus.

1   Rewrite this paragraph, which starts — and should remain — in the past tense.

Many years ago in a distant land, crocodiles were plentiful in the rivers. An elderly crocodile, who is beginning to feel weak, believes that he would regain his strength if he can eat a monkey's heart. Accordingly, he asks his son to bring him one.

2   Rewrite this paragraph, which starts — and should remain — in the present tense.

David is strolling across a field one sunny morning when he noticed a bird stumbling awkwardly as it tried to run away from him. It was dragging the feathers of one wing over the ground, while it flapped the other wing. Wishing to help the poor bird, which appeared to be hurt, David hurried after it.

32 The joining words 'who', 'which' and 'that'

We use 'who' when referring to people. We use 'which' or 'that' when referring to things or to animals.

The girl came from India. She was welcomed to the school.
The girl, **who** came from India, was welcomed to the school.

The dress was bought last week. The dress has shrunk
The dress, **which** was bought last week, has shrunk.

Note: We can use 'that' in place of 'whom' when referring to people.

The man **that** the police were looking for is dead. (Notice that when we use 'that', no commas are necessary.)

Join these pairs of sentences in the same way.

1 Steven is a clever boy. He has been chosen for the quiz.
2 The beaver is a hard-working animal. It is a native of Canada.
3 Mrs Brown won the tournament. She plays every day.
4 The jet was grounded. It had engine trouble.

33 Plural nouns

Write each of the sentences below, using the plural form of the verb unless the singular aspect of the word is indicated by using 'a pair of'.

1 The tongs (were was) by the fireplace.
2 A pair of scissors (is are) in the drawer.
3 The garden shears (was were) used to clip the hedge.
4 A pair of trousers (are is) hanging in the cupboard.
5 Tweezers (are is) useful when handling stamps.

34 Make your sentences simple

Rewrite the sentences below, cutting out these impersonal or pompous words:

should circumstances arise that (Use 'if'.)
it is often the case that (Use 'often'.)
it is to be regretted that (Use 'unfortunately'.)
it should be obvious that (Use 'of course'.)

1 Tom is doing well, and it should be obvious that he must go to university.
2 It is to be regretted that we cannot have you to stay.
3 Should circumstances arise that work becomes available, we shall tell you.
4 We find that it is often the case that children who cannot read well have poor eyesight.

35 Euphemisms

In the sentences, below, the euphemisms in bold type are used in speech to gloss over unpleasant facts. When writing, it is better to be more direct.

Write each sentence, using one word instead of each euphemism.

1 The boy next door is a **little careless of the truth**.
2 My uncle was **under the weather** when he came home.
3 Old Tom is **pushing up the daisies**.
4 Aunt Bess has become **hard of hearing** lately.
5 The boys like to **bend the elbow** after playing rugby.
6 The boss said that Jim was **no longer required**.

36 Singular pronouns require singular verbs

The pronouns **another, anything, each, everyone, everybody anyone, someone, somebody, no one, either and neither** are singular.

Use the correct form of the verb in brackets when you write these sentences.

1 Everyone in the class (to have) handed in work.
2 Neither of the girls (to seem) to be correct.
3 Each of the boys (to be) given a medal yesterday.
4 Either of the girls (to like) to drive the tractor now.

37 Words that are out of order

In these sentences, change the order of the words so that they will make sense. You will also have to add commas.

1 Brian made a spinning wheel entirely from his head for Mother.
2 Uncle Allan praised his granddaughter who is over ninety.
3 The basin was carried by a girl full of soapy water.
4 Mavis put a complete coat of paint on herself.
5 The boy wrote to the Queen who lives next door.

38 Making one sentence by joining with a present participle

The thief cut through the padlock. He opened the wooden door.
Cutting through the padlock, the thief opened the wooden door.

Join each pair of sentences below, using a present participle.

1 The pilot banked sharply. She managed to avoid the buildings.
2 He disguised himself as a cleaner. He entered the bank.
3 She drove as quickly as possible. She arrived just in time.
4 The lightning flashed vividly. It struck the church steeple.

39 Vary your sentences by beginning with a phrase

Rewrite these sentences, placing the phrases at the beginning.
Remember to use commas where necessary.

1   A shed was damaged during the storm.
2   They could not explore the cave without a torch.
3   A shiny, black revolver lay under the bag.
4   The crickets began their piercing calls at nightfall.

40 Four ways to join clauses

A   I joined the team; everyone was so friendly.
B   I joined the team and everyone was so friendly.
C   When I joined the team, everyone was so friendly.
D   Everyone was so friendly when I joined the team.

Join these pairs of clauses, using the models as directed.

1   (*Use model A*) He opened the door. The stranger walked inside.
2   (*Use model B*) Frank lit the fire. The room became warmer.
3   (*Use model C*) The neighbours moved. New tenants arrived from Darwin.
4   (*Use model D*) Several friends were invited. I gave a party.

41 Unclear sentences

Rewrite each sentence below, making the meaning clear by changing the order of the words. Remember to add commas if necessary.

1   He wore a hat on his head made of coconut fibre.
2   I noticed a wallaby walking to school this morning.
3   Dad announced that he was building a factory after lunch.
4   James sat next to the dog talking to himself.
5   She bought a chair from the woman with wobbly legs.

42 For variety, use a phrase or an adverb to begin a sentence

I visited Cairns during the winter.
During the winter, I visited Cairns.

The dog looked hungrily at the meat pie.
Hungrily the dog looked at the meat pie.

Rewrite the sentences below, varying them in this way.

1 My mother cooked a meal after the show.
2 He staggered wearily along the dusty road
3 We saw a flashing light in the distance.
4 I stupidly trod on a sleeping snake.

43 Making one sentence by joining with a past participle

The car was damaged in the accident. It needed a new door.
Damaged in the accident, the car needed a new door.

Rewrite the sentences below, joining each pair in this way.

1 The boat was tossed up and down. It developed a leak.
2 The girls were aroused by the dog. They knew someone
   was around.
3 I was impressed by the team. I stayed for the whole match.
4 She was pleased with her present. She gave him a hug.

44 Overworked words — 'went'

Write each sentence below, using a word from the box in place
of the one in brackets.

stormed	travelled	bolted	hopped	crawled	charged

1 The angry bull (went) across the paddock.
2 A kangaroo (went) across the road in front of us.
3 Feeling annoyed, the speaker (went) from the hall.
4 Frightened by a noise, the horse suddenly (went) up the hill.
5 We (went) in a large paddle steamer.
6 Up his bare arm (went) the hairy caterpillar.

45 One way of combining three sentences into one

The pilot lost much blood. He struggled with the controls. They felt sluggish.

Having lost much blood, the pilot struggled with the controls, which felt sluggish.

Make one sentence from each group of three below, using the same construction as the example above.

1 The boy walked home. He met his friend William. William had been playing football.
2 I climbed the ladder. I helped the child down. He had been too frightened to move.
3 The crocodile swam closer. It grabbed the bait. The bait was on the end of a line.

46 Some expressions take singular verbs

Some common expressions take singular verbs even though they may contain a plural noun.

Write these sentences, using the singular form of the verbs.

1 Bacon and eggs (were was) served for breakfast.
2 Where (is are) the cheese and biscuits?
3 Fish and chips (is are) popular in England.

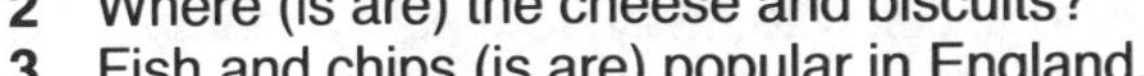

47 Useful words that link sentences

in addition	in the same way	similarly	for instance

The man was charged with breaking and entering. **In addition**, he was suspected of comitting a serious crime in another state.

Link each pair of sentences below by using a word or phrase from the box to begin the second sentence.

1   I believe that smoking is a very dangerous habit. Have you thought of the many people who die from cancer because they smoke?

2   Ivor Iron, the professional golfer, played badly. He was extremely rude to a press photographer.

3   The camel lives in desert regions and has adapted itself by growing a hump to store fat to live on when there is nothing to eat. The giraffe has grown a long neck, which enables it to eat leaves from tall trees.

4   Stanley Matthews was a great footballer who used his quick reflexes to stop suddenly when running with the ball. He used his reflexes to accelerate away from his opponent.

48 Conversation words that should not be written

These words or phrases, used in ordinary conversation, have the more formal meaning written alongside.

tough luck — unfortunate   have a go — try

rip off — defraud   dicey — risky

a piece of cake — easy   play up — misbehave

Rewrite these sentences, using the formal or standard English word instead of the slang or conversational phrase or word.

1   Some people on the dole try to rip off the system.
2   Steven is always playing up at school.
3   I shall have a go to win the squash championship.
4   It was tough luck that she fell close to the finishing line.
5   The burglar thought it was a piece of cake to open the safe.
6   It is dicey to ride a bike at night with no lights.

49 Correcting mistakes

Rewrite the sentences, changing the form of the underlined pronouns, which are incorrect.

1   Wendy and <u>me</u> went to the show.
2   <u>Her</u> and Jane both go to my school.
3   The perfume is for your sister and <u>yourself</u>.
4   <u>Him</u> and his brother are good swimmers.
5   Skiing was new to Charles and I.
6   <u>Us</u> boys decided to go for a ride.

50 Position of the word 'even'

The word 'even' should be written in front of and next to the word it modifies.

Rewrite each sentence, putting in the word 'even' to give the meaning described in brackets.

1   Alice could not see the bird in the picture (Alice, let alone anyone else, could not see it)
2   Alice could not see the bird in the picture. (Alice could not see other things, let alone the bird)
3   Alice could not see the bird in the picture. (Alice could not see the bird, let alone the one in the picture)

51 Use the right prepositions with these phrases

Write the sentences, below, using the correct preposition.

1   Her new shoes are quite different (to from than) mine.
2   Danny will benefit (by with from) the experience.
3   Mathew is capable (of to with) doing better.
4   My sister has the opportunity (at to of) travelling to Japan.

52 Change of tense

The first verb in a sentence establishes the tense of any verb that comes later. The second verb in these sentences has a change of tense. Rewrite each sentence so that the second verb is the same tense as the first.

1   In the story, the hero loses all his money, but everything came right at the end.
2   The team won last Saturday but goes and loses this afternoon.
3   Dad went to the hotel for a while and returns with a friend.
4   Maureen uses a small toothbrush so that it reached her back teeth.

53 Useful words that link sentences

> by contrast,   instead,   as a result,   meanwhile,
> despite this,   in this case

Write each pair of sentences below. In each case, use a word or a phrase from the box to begin the second sentence. Notice that four of the sentences are separated by semicolons. Use a comma after each phrase.

1   The man was convicted of speeding previously. He should not have exceeded the limit again.
2   Mary was given the best medical attention; she died soon after.
3   The people in Switzerland work hard; Australians are considered to be lazy.
4   Mrs Jones went on a strict diet; she lost five kilograms.
5   Mavis decided not to receive a present; she accepted a cheque from her parents.
6   The camper was sleeping peacefully on the river bank. A crocodile came creeping closer.

54 Unclear sentences

Rewrite each sentences below, adding a comma to make the meaning clear.

1   In the evening paper darts were made.
2   Shall we walk on Donald?
3   As far as I know the poem is an old one.
4   I shall spend time shooting at my uncle's home.
5   While Joan was eating her finger felt numb.
6   As it turned out the rabbit was tame.

55 More groups of words to avoid which repeat one idea

The underlined words in the groups below can be left out.

check <u>up on</u>   miss <u>out on</u>   separate <u>out</u>

meet <u>with</u>   end <u>up</u>   <u>as</u> from

Rewrite these sentences, which contain repeated ideas.

1   There will be no more biology lessons this term, as from Monday.
2   Will you please separate out the good tennis balls from the worn ones.
3   If we do not hurry, we shall miss out on the film.
4   I must look at the docket and check up on the total.
5   Are you able to meet with me in the morning?
6   That boy will end up in jail.

56 A plural noun that names a single object

When a group of words containing a plural noun represents a single object, you must use a singular verb.

'The Adventures of Tom Sawyer' was enjoyed by us all.

Write these sentences using the correct form of the verb. Be careful, because you must use the plural form in one example.

1 'Tales of the South Pacific' (were was) exciting.
2 'The Crusades' is a book that (come comes) in two volumes.
3 Robert Louis Stevenson's books (is are) always exciting.
4 'Memories of the War' (is are) worth reading.

57 More euphemisms

Rewrite each sentence, using one a word instead of each euphemism in bold type. The euphemism is used to gloss over an upleasant fact.

1 My grandmother **passed on** last week.
2 His father is becoming **thin on top**.
3 The woman next door has just had a **visit from the stork**.
4 Linda has become **overweight** because she eats too much.
5 The workers decided to **take industrial action**.
6 Clothing was collected for the **disadvantaged** in the city.

58 Use the right preposition

Write these sentences, choosing the correct words from the brackets.

1 Sharon was suffering (with from) a cold.
2 Riding is preferable (than to) walking.
3 Helen is fed up (of with) being beaten at tennis.
4 Her hat was adorned (by with) feathers.
5 The weather is a change (to for) the better.

59 Word order to create emphasis

Least emphatic: Christian planned mutiny in order to escape.
More emphatic: Mutiny was Christian's plan in order to escape.
Most emphatic: Christian had a plan in order to escape —
mutiny.

Change these *least emphatic* sentences to more emphatic and most emphatic (write six sentences altogether.) Remember to add commas, if necessary.

1   He knew <u>torture</u> awaited him if he was captured.
2   They thought about <u>water</u> all the time.
3   The pilot knew <u>hijacking</u> was one possibility.

60 Group words take singular or plural verbs

Group words, or collective nouns, take a singular verb if you are talking of the group as a whole. They take a plural verb if you are talking about individuals within the group.

The team **is** on the field. The team **are** changing or showering.
The class **is** a bright one. The class **are** a mixed lot.

Use 'is' or 'are' to complete these sentences.

1   His family . . . living in that house.
2   His family . . . living in various parts of Sydney.
3   The jury . . . in the courtroom.
4   The jury . . . still debating the case.

61 Correcting mistakes

Correct these sentences by changing the form of the underlined verb.

1   My father has <u>laid</u> in bed all day.
2   Each of the girls <u>were</u> at the party.
3   A jar of lollies <u>are</u> on the table.
4   Both mare and foal <u>feeds</u> together.
5   Neither of the boys <u>are</u> playing well.
6   Mother has <u>lain</u> the book down somewhere.

62 Incomplete constructions

One or more words can be omitted when they are clearly implied.

> The girls had eaten and gone to the cinema. (Instead of 'the girls had eaten and had gone to the cinema'.)

Errors can occur when the verb that is implied cannot be used.

> The dogs have been groomed and the kennel washed. (*wrong*)
> The dogs have been groomed and the kennel has been washed. (*right, because the verb must be changed*)

Correct these sentences:

1 The girl was beaten and future games cancelled.
2 His horse was first and the other two second and third.
3 The floor has been cleaned and the dishes washed.
4 Jones is to be a winger and Smith and Brown forwards.

63 'When' and 'where'

These words cannot introduce noun clauses.

> Puberty is when a person is able to produce offspring. (*wrong*)
> Puberty is the condition of a person who is able to produce offspring. (*right*)

> Erosion is where wind wears the rock away. (*wrong*)
> Erosion occurs where the wind wears the rock away. (*right*)

Correct these sentences using the same construction as those above.

1 Illiteracy is when a person is unable to read or write.
2 Pollution is where the environment is spoiled by man-made waste.

64 Historic present

When writing about the past, we can use the present tense to make it appear as if an event is actually happening. Even if a person is dead, he or she can still be spoken of in the present tense. This is known as using the **historic present**.

Nelson is one of England's greatest admirals.
In 1666 the Great Fire of London breaks out.

Rewrite these sentences, using the historic present.

1 The landing at Gallipoli was a special event in Australian history.
2 Banjo Patterson was one of our greatest writers.
3 Robert Menzies ranked as a great prime minister.
4 Captain Cook was responsible for white settlement in Australia.

65 Adjective or adverb?

Write each sentence below, using one of the words in brackets.

1 She decided to walk (easy easily).
2 The team played (real really) well in the first half.
3 My sister plays (fair fairly) at cards.
4 Donald is a (fair fairly) squash player.

66 More nouns that always need a plural verb

Write each sentence below using the plural form of the verb unless the singular aspect of the word is indicated by using 'a pair of'.

1 The binoculars (is are) handy at the races.
2 His new glasses (was were) on the dining room table.
3 Bring me the pair of knickers that (is are) on the line.
4 A pair of pyjamas (was were) in the bottom drawer.

67 Use of the article 'a'

The article 'a' placed in front of a noun conveys the idea of 'one'. When writing about two separate objects, a second 'a' must be used. If two objects are considered as one, then the second 'a' may be left out.

I have a hammer and a chisel. (*two separate objects*)
The mechanic used a block and tackle to lift the engine. (*one object*)

Write these sentences using the article 'a' correctly.

1   You will need (a) saw and (a) drill.
2   The fisherman was using (a) rod and (a) reel.
3   This is (a) gravy and (a) sauce dish.
4   For camping you must take (a) sleeping bag and (a) frying pan.

68 Active and passive verbs

It is generally better and more effective to use active rather than passive verbs.

Passive: The Aborigines were treated badly by early settlers.
Active: The early settlers treated the Aborigines badly.

Rewrite each sentence below, making the verbs active.

1   The news of her death was received by me with sadness.
2   A high standard was set by the athletes.
3   The note was written by someone at school.
4   An office is being built on the site.
5   Your help will be appreciated by us.
6   The hotel is being painted by a contractor.

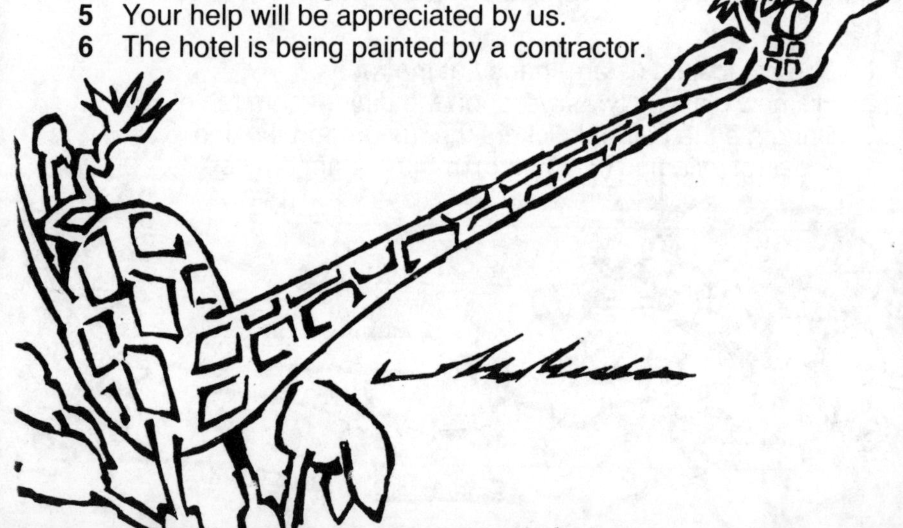

69 Run-on sentences

The run-on sentence is a common fault. It is really two separate sentences that have been joined with a comma instead of a colon, a full stop or a joining word.

The giraffe is an ungainly animal, it has such a long neck.

This could be written:

The giraffe is an ungainly animal; it has such a long neck.
The giraffe is an ungainly animal. It has such a long neck.
The giraffe is an ungainly animal which has a long neck.
The giraffe is an ungainly animal in that it has such a long neck.

Correct the run-on sentence below in four ways.

Columbus was a great navigator, he knew the world was round.

70 Write comparisons clearly

Below are four examples of comparisons that are unclear. Write each one correctly, by changing one word or using as few extra words as possible.

1   The grapes grown in Australia are better than in France.
2   Harold is the strongest of the two brothers.
3   Steven likes Donald better than Michael.
4   Einstein was cleverer than any man.

71 Make your sentences simple

Rewrite the sentences below, cutting out these unnecessary phrases:

owing to the fact that (use 'because')
is one who (omit)
concerning the matter of (use 'about')
by means of (use 'by')
regardless of the fact that (use 'although')
in this day and age (use 'today')

1   The principal wants to see you concerning the matter of the broken window.
2   I was late owing the fact that the train broke down.
3   In this day and age we should all use calculators.
4   We may yet travel to the stars by means of nuclear-powered rockets.
5   She is one who likes dancing to that kind of music.

72 More conversation words that should not be written

wipe out — fail   get the message — understand

send up — mimic   capers — mischief

fantastic — very enjoyable   clean up — make a profit

Rewrite these sentences, using the formal or standard English word instead of the slang or conversational phrase or word.

1 His father cleaned up when he opened a used-car yard.
2 I got the message why Father was so annoyed.
3 The twins were always into capers after school.
4 The skit is designed to send up 'Countdown'.
5 I was wiped out at the end of the first year in my course.
6 We had a fantastic time at the party.

73 When a singular verb is needed

Six months was a long time to be away. (The verb agrees with 'a long time'.)
Ten kilometres is a long way to walk. (The verb agrees with 'a long way'.)
Petrol or kerosene is used. (Two singular nouns joined by 'or' take a singular verb.)

Grapes or a melon is suitable. (Here the verb agrees with the nearest noun — it would be better to use the plural noun second; then a plural verb would be used.)

One of the calves is sick. (A singular verb is used after 'one of' and a plural noun.)

Write each sentence below, using the correct form of the verb.

1 Bullets or a bomb (is are) not allowed on the plane.
2 One of our men (was were) injured in the crash.
3 Fifty dollars (is are) too much to lose.
4 Jam or butter (was were) not available to the prisoners.

74 Do not change person when using pronouns

When writing, you may use pronouns from each of three groups.

First person — **I, we**
Second person — **you**
Third person — **he, she, they, one, anyone, everyone**

Do not change from one group to another, as has been done in the sentences below. Rewrite the sentences correctly.

1   If you want to play tennis well, one must practise.
2   I enjoy swimming, because you feel refreshed afterwards.
3   If girls study and they want to become doctors, we can.
4   Some people feel that when they leave school you are
    entitled to the dole.

75   Avoid sentence fragments

A complete sentence must make sense by itself. A fragment is a sentence that is not complete. It is often a phrase or a clause that belongs to the sentence before it. Rewrite this paragraph correctly.

We were lucky to see the kangaroo. Hiking through the scrub. It was sitting quietly. With only its ears moving. Daniel motioned me to keep still. While he focused his camera. Suddenly the animal bounded away. An example of the shy nature of the kangaroo.

76 'Like' and 'without'

'Like' is either a verb or preposition. 'Without' is a preposition. Neither of these words can be used as a conjunction.

> That girl writes like I do. (*wrong — 'like' is used as a conjunction*)
> That girl writes as I do. (*right*)

> We cannot play without he gives us permission. (*wrong — 'without' is used as a conjunction*)
> We cannot play unless he gives us permission. (*right*)

Correct these sentences. Choose between the conjunctions 'as' and 'unless' in the first two examples. In the third, use 'like' as a preposition and omit the second verb and its subject.

1   He will not come without I tell him.
2   My brother walks like she does.
3   The man looks like he is a professional.

77 Parallel construction

Your writing will be clearer if you use parallel construction. When you list items, they should be in similar form.

> Mother likes sewing, painting and to play tennis. (*not parallel*)
> Mother likes sewing, painting and playing tennis. (*parallel*)

Read each example below and decide if the construction is parallel or not. Write P or NP next to your numbers.

1   I swept the yard, weeded the garden and then there was the washing up to be done.
2   The new player is strong, clever and intelligent.
3   Although I trained hard, practised each day, and I listened to my coach, I never won a tornament.
4   I only eat lean meat, I rarely eat chips, and I never touch chocolate.

78 Unclear sentences

Rewrite each sentence, making the meaning clear by changing the order of the words.

1   Brian won the walking race for three years running.
2   Mr Smith saw a fox looking out of the window of the coach.
3   Mother cooked a meal for the visitor made of scraps.
4   Daniel's hair needs cutting badly.
5   My grandfather is fond of eating oysters and old leather chairs.
6   He telephoned asking me to come next Sunday today.

79 Making one sentence from two, using 'whom' and 'whose'

The boy is very tall. We swam in his pool.
The body, in whose pool we swam, is very tall.

Make one sentence from each of the pairs below, choosing the correct pair of words from the box. Remember to use commas if necessary.

from whom	beside whom	with whom
to whom	on whose	

1   I played golf with a visitor. He was a good player.
2   We sat beside a woman. The woman was your aunt.
3   I rode on Harry's horse. Harry watched me closely.
4   She received a letter from a boy. She knew the boy at school
5   I sent a parcel to my friend. He received it yesterday.

80 Correcting mistakes

In each sentence below, change the underlined word to make the sentence correct.

1 Have you read <u>where</u> there was an earthquake in Greece?
2 She shared the chips <u>between</u> the three girls.
3 The dog waited <u>besides</u> the front gate.
4 A bus runs <u>passed</u> our house.
5 I must <u>of</u> left my purse at home.
6 She is the <u>most</u> agressive of the two.

81 'Shall' and 'will'

Simple future — I shall, we shall, you will, he will, she will, they will

Showing determination — I will, we will, you shall, he shall, she shall, they shall

I **shall** be leaving soon.　　I **will** not obey you.

Use the correct word from the brackets to complete each sentance below.

1 We (will shall) be going on holidays next week.
2 I (will shall) be in Israel next month.
3 We (will shall) never surrender. (*determination*)
4 She (will shall) be travelling by bus in future.
5 He (will shall) be at university soon.
6 I (will shall) try even harder. (*determination*)

82 Using the right pronoun

Complete each sentence, choosing the correct word from the brackets.

1   Dianna is one player (who whom) may beat me.
2   I cannot bear the thought of (his him) leaving.
3   An argument developed between his sister and (he him).
4   Do you think it is (they them) who have arrived?
5   Jane is the person (who whom) I think spoke to you.
6   We knew we were as strong as (they them).

83 Absolute adjective

These adjectives are absolute and cannot be compared:

entirely	unique	round	square
perfect	opposite	empty	dead

Rewrite these sentences correctly. (One does not need to be changed.)

1   She wore a very perfect diamond on her finger.
2   His garden is extremely square.
3   This is a very ancient monument.
4   He had a very unique Chinese vase on the desk.

84 Correcting mistakes

In each sentence below, change the underlined word to make the sentence correct.

1   Will you <u>leave</u> go my dress.
2   Maria asked him <u>if</u> he was happy.
3   <u>Without</u> it snows, we cannot ski tomorrow.
4   <u>Aside</u> from Martina, I have not seen a stronger player.
5   Neither Bill <u>or</u> Dennis can bat well.
6   He drove fast so <u>as</u> he might arrive early.

Answers

Exercise 1

1   Does Sharon now make models from clay?
2   Does David go to school by train?
3   Do the children practise the violin each morning?
4   Did our team play well yesterday?

Exercise 2

1   My brother earned two hundred dollars a week.
2   In the first half, the winger scored a try.
3   While holidaying in Toronto, Terry acquired a strong Canadian accent.
4   She coaxed the cat to eat some of the fish.
5   In the jungle, many of the men became sick.
6   Luckily she caught the last train from Sydney.

Exercise 3

1   Shocked as she was, she could not find her way.
2   Up flew the frightened bird.
3   For myself, I would like only his old photograph.
4   Unceasingly the guns boomed out.

Exercise 4

1   When the children went to the zoo, they saw a baby koala.
2   We can go to the park when the weather clears.
3   Everybody went home when the game finished.
4   It is dark in this room when the lights are turned off.

Exercise 5

1   Camouflaged torpedo boats were anchored in the tiny cove.
2   Lumbering dinosaurs roamed the earth at that time.
3   Experienced players are needed for the tour of England.
4   Interesting books filled the shelves of her study.

Exercise 6

1   'Help! Help!' shrieked the frightened child.
2   Nearer and nearer came the figure dressed in black.
3   Down, down sank the torpedoed ship.
4   Bang! Bang! went the pistol as he took careful aim.

Exercise 7

1 The police arrived first and the ambulance came soon after.
2 Their front door was open, but nobody was at home.
3 His rope was thin, but it was very strong.
4 Donald took out his pen and began to make notes.

Exercise 8

1 Tomorrow the tennis matches will start.
2 Outside, the strong wind howled.
3 Sometimes koalas grunt.
4 Wildly, Paul rushed into the room.

Exercise 9

1 We all swam at the beach yesterday.
2 Have you written to thank your aunt?
3 William drank all the ginger beer.
4 The bell for school has already rung.
5 The cow has trodden on my sweet peas.
6 Her new shorts shrank after a week.

Exercise 10

1 The brave soldiers attacked at dawn.
2 Several wild dogs came close.
3 The very strong wind sprang up suddenly.
4 The painfully hot sun beat down on the horsemen.

Exercise 11

1 Susan will probably lose because she is making many mistakes. The loser will probably be Susan, who is making many mistakes.
2 One pupil, who is very gifted, will probably be a painter. The painter will probably be the pupil who is very gifted.

Exercise 12

1 May I go to the pictures after lunch, Mother?
2 Can you come here and hold the ladder?
3 May I come in?

Exercise 13

1 He has nothing to declare at the airport.
2 Megan can hardly wait until her birthday.
3 There was nobody at the front door.
4 They had scarcely enough feed for their cattle.

Exercise 14

1   The crocodiles snapped angrily at the boat in the river.
2   A man in a black coat suddenly appeared.
3   A gang of hoodlums stood in front of my brother.
4   The castle on the mountain was heavily bombed during the war.

Exercise 15

1   Four pupils from our school entered the local swimming carnival.
2   One person who never reached the finals was Stephanie.
3   Judith came fourth in the 200 metres freestyle final.
4   The 100 metres backstroke was won by Arnold.

Exercise 16

1   She carefully unscrewed the lid with some pliers.
2   Houses near the beach were damaged by the waves.
3   Flags of many nations waved proudly in the breeze.
4   The boys on bicycles delivered pamphlets to every house.

Exercise 17

1   There were fewer children in the class than expected.
2   We were given less work today than yesterday.
3   The use of seat belts in cars has led to fewer fatalities.

Exercise 18

1   The team did not play too well last season.
2   We have not picked nearly enough yet.
3   My grandmother was walking slowly past.
4   Come to my house as quickly as possible.
5   We had a really excellent time at the party.
6   Sharon won her race easily.

Exercise 19

1   Dad has lain on the sofa all morning.
2   Marjorie says she has already laid the table.
3   The book was laid on the chest of drawers.
4   I would like to lie in the sun this morning.
5   While lying in bed, I had an idea.
6   Each day she lays her books neatly on the desk.

Exercise 20

1 I like these kinds of apples.
2 Do you prefer this sort of meat pie?
3 That kind of coffee is sold everywhere.
4 Those are the kinds of days I like.
5 These types of cars are very fast.
6 This class of animal is rare.

Exercise 21

1 Mother cooked some pasta which was delicious.
2 In the lounge room were tasteful curtains.
3 He wore some fragrant perfume to the disco.
4 The three days in Fiji were enjoyable.
5 I think the male vocalist is handsome.
6 My uncle is always kind to visitors.

Exercise 22

1 Only David may sleep on the bed.
2 David may sleep only on the bed.
3 David may sleep on the only bed.
4 David may only sleep on the bed.

Exercise 23

1 The dog, hungry and exhausted, lay in the gutter. The dog, which was hungry and exhausted, lay in the gutter.
2 A spike, sharp and pointed, had been driven into the ground. A spike, which was sharp and pointed, had been driven into the ground.

Exercise 24

1 His old car goes quickly but sounds noisy.
2 She held the money tightly even though her arm hurt badly.
3 Did you do well in the test after not feeling well?

Exercise 25

1 The ship rocked violently in the storm. In the storm, the ship rocked violently. Violently the ship rocked in the storm. The ship in the storm rocked violently.
2 The artist worked painstakingly at his masterpiece. At his masterpiece, the artist worked painstakingly. Painstakingly, the artist worked at his masterpiece. The artist painstakingly worked at his masterpiece.

46

Exercise 26

1 We bought some lemons from which we extracted the juice.
2 Steven lent me a mattress on which I slept soundly.
3 I picked up a stick, with which I killed the snake.
4 There was a towbar on the car, to which we attached the trailer.
5 My aunt gave me a sewing machine for which I was very grateful.
6 The plane was comfortable in which we travelled. The plane in which we travelled was comfortable.

Exercise 27

1 Dad was offered a gift by the firm.
2 We continued to the next village.
3 The dog followed the rabbit into the hole.
4 Her car was here until this morning.
5 The river was brown after the rains.
6 A plate fell from the shelf.
7 You will need to refer to the previous page.

Exercise 28

1 Cruising in the glass-bottomed boat, we could see many kinds of fish.
2 We gave to the geese all the scraps that were ready to throw away.
3 She left on the counter the bread that was too hard to eat.
4 I bought a clock with crooked hands from the dealer.
5 Flying at a thousand feet, I could see the mountain clearly.
6 I read in the paper that the burglar had been caught.

Exercise 29

1 Neither Robert nor I have been to the opera.
2 The farmer offered Susan and me a job.
3 I can swim as fast as she.
4 He thinks that we two can win the doubles match.
5 Between you and me there are few secrets.
6 Both he and I are going to the beach.

Exercise 30

1 I am uncertain what to take when I leave for Japan.
2 I shall take my brother with me when I go.
3 Shall I take her a cup of tea in bed?
4 Bring that book to me at my desk.

Exercise 31

1   Many years ago in a distant land, crocodiles were plentiful in the rivers. An elderly crocodile, who was beginning to feel weak, believed that he would regain his strength if he could eat a monkey's heart. Accordingly, he asked his son to bring him one.
2   David is strolling across a field one sunny morning when he notices a bird stumbling awkwardly as it tries to run away from him. It is dragging the feathers of one wing over the ground, while it flaps the other wing. Wishing to help the poor bird, which appears to be hurt, David hurries after it.

Exercise 32

1   Steven, who is a clever boy, has been chosen for the quiz.
2   The beaver, which is a hard-working animal, is a native of Canada.
3   Mrs Brown, who plays every day, won the tournament.
4   The jet, which was grounded, had engine trouble. The jet that was grounded had engine trouble.

Exercise 33

1   The tongs were by the fireplace.
2   A pair of scissors is in the drawer.
3   The garden shears were used to clip the hedge.
4   A pair of trousers is hanging in the cupboard.
5   Tweezers are useful when handling stamps.

Exercise 34

1   Tom is doing well, and of course he must go to university.
2   Unfortunately we cannot have you to stay.
3   If work becomes available, we shall tell you.
4   We find that often children who cannot read have poor eyesight.

Exercise 35

1   The boy next door is a liar.
2   My uncle was drunk when he came home.
3   Old Tom is dead.
4   Aunt Bess has become deaf lately.
5   The boys like to drink after playing rugby.
6   The boss said that Jim was fired.

Exercise 36

1   Everyone in the class has handed in work.
2   Neither of the girls seems to be correct.
3   Each of the boys was given a medal yesterday.
4   Either of the girls likes to drive the tractor now.

Exercise 37

1   Brian, entirely from his head, made a spinning wheel for Mother.
2   Uncle Allan, who is over ninety, praised his granddaughter.
3   The basin, full of soapy water, was carried by a girl.
4   Mavis, herself, put on a complete coat of paint. ('Mavis, herself, put a complete coat of paint on' ends with preposition, so is not considered grammatically correct.)
5   The boy, who lives next door, wrote to the Queen.

Exercise 38

1   Banking sharply, the pilot managed to avoid the buildings.
2   Disguising himself as a cleaner, he entered the bank.
3   Driving as quickly as possible, she arrived just in time.
4   Flashing vividly, the lightning struck the church steeple.

Exercise 39

1   During the storm, a shed was damaged.
2   Without a torch, they could not explore the cave.
3   Under the bag lay a shiny, black revolver.
4   At nightfall, the crickets began their piercing calls.

Exercise 40

1   He opened the door; the stranger walked inside.
2   Frank lit the fire and the room became warmer.
3   When the neighbours moved, new tenants arrived from Darwin.
4   Several friends were invited when I gave a party.

Exercise 41

1   He wore on his head a hat made of coconut fibre.
2   Walking to school this morning, I noticed a wallaby.
3   Dad announced, after lunch, that he was building a factory. After lunch, Dad announced that he was building a factory.
4   James sat talking to himself next to the dog.
5   She bought a chair with wobbly legs from the woman.

Exercise 42

1   After the show, my mother cooked a meal.
2   Along the dusty road he staggered wearily.
3   In the distance we saw a flashing light.
4   Stupidly I trod on a sleeping snake.

Exercise 43

1   Tossed up and down, the boat developed a leak.
2   Aroused by the dog, the girls knew someone was around.
3   Impressed by the team, I stayed for the whole match.
4   Pleased with her present, she gave him a hug.

Exercise 44

1   The angry bull charged across the paddock.
2   A kangaroo hopped across the road in front of us.
3   Feeling annoyed, the speaker stormed from the hall.
4   Frightened by a noise, the horse suddenly bolted up the hill.
5   We travelled in a large paddle steamer.
6   Up his bare arm crawled the hairy caterpillar.

Exercise 45

1   Having walked home, the boy met his friend William, who
    had been playing football.
2   Having climbed the ladder, I helped the child down who had
    been too frightened to move.
3   Having swum closer, the crocodile grabbed the bait, which
    was on the end of the line.

Exercise 46

1   Bacon and eggs was served for breakfast.
2   Where is the cheese and biscuits?
3   Fish and chips is popular in England.

Exercise 47

1   I believe that smoking is a very dangerous habit. For instance, have you thought of the many people who die from cancer because they smoke?
2   Ivor Iron, the professional golfer, played badly. In addition, he was extremely rude to a press photographer.
3   The camel lives in desert regions and has adapted itself by growing a hump to store fat to live on when there is nothing to eat. Similarly, the giraffe has grown a long neck, which enables it to eat leaves from tall trees.
4   Stanley Matthews was a great footballer who used his quick reflexes to stop suddenly when running with the ball. In the same way, he used his reflexes to accelerate away from his opponent.

Exercise 48

1   Some people on the dole try to defraud the system.
2   Steven is always misbehaving at school.
3   I shall try to win the squash championship.
4   It was unfortunate that she fell close to the finishing line.
5   The burglar thought it was easy to open the safe.
6   It is risky to ride a bike at night with no lights.

Exercise 49

1   Wendy and I went to the show.
2   She and Jane both go to my school.
3   The perfume is for your sister and you.
4   He and his brother are good swimmers.
5   Skiing was new to Charles and me.
6   We boys decided to go for a ride.

Exercise 50

1   Even Alice could not see the bird in the picture.
2   Alice could not even see the bird in the picture.
3   Alice could not see even the bird in the picture.

Exercise 51

1   Her new shoes are quite different from mine.
2   Danny will benefit from the experience.
3   Mathew is capable of doing better.
4   My sister has the opportunity of travelling to Japan.

Exercise 52

1 In the story, the hero loses all his money, but everything comes right in the end.
2 The team won last Saturday but went and lost this afternoon.
3 Dad went to the hotel for a while and returned with a friend.
4 Maureen uses a small toothbrush so that it reaches her back teeth.

Exercise 53

1 The man was convicted of speeding previously. In this case, he should not have exceeded the limit again.
2 Mary was given the best medical attention; despite this, she died soon after.
3 The people in Switzerland work hard; by contrast, Australians are considered to be lazy.
4 Mrs Jones went on a strict diet; as a result, she lost five kilograms.
5 Mavis decided not to receive a present; instead, she accepted a cheque from her parents.
6 The camper was sleeping peacefully on the river bank. Meanwhile, a crocodile came creeping closer.

Exercise 54

1 In the evening, paper darts were made.
2 Shall we walk on, Donald?
3 As far as I know, the poem is an old one.
4 I shall spend time shooting, at my uncle's home.
5 While Joan was eating, her finger felt numb.
6 As it turned out, the rabbit was tame.

Exercise 55

1 There will be no more biology lessons this term, from Monday.
2 Will you please separate the good tennis balls from the worn ones.
3 If we do not hurry, we shall miss the film.
4 I must look at the docket and check the total.
5 Are you able to meet me in the morning?
6 That boy will end in jail.

Exercise 56

1 'Tales of the South Pacific' was exciting.
2 'The Crusades' is a book that comes in two volumes.
3 Robert Louis Stevenson's books are always exciting.
4 'Memories of the War' is worth reading.

Exercise 57

1 My grandmother died last week.
2 His father is becoming bald.
3 The woman next door has just had a baby.
4 Linda has become fat because she eats too much.
5 The workers decided to strike.
6 Clothing was collected for the poor in the city.

Exercise 58

1 Sharon was suffering from a cold.
2 Riding is preferable to walking.
3 Helen is fed up with being beaten at tennis.
4 Her hat was adorned with feathers.
5 The weather is a change for the better.

Exercise 59

1 Torture, he knew, awaited him if he was captured. He knew what waited for him if he was captured — torture.
2 Water was what they thought about all the time. They thought about it all the time — water.
3 Hijacking was a possibility, the pilot knew. The pilot knew a possibility was — hijacking.

Exercise 60

1 His family is living in that house.
2 His family are living in various parts of Sydney.
3 The jury is in the courtroom.
4 The jury are still debating the case.

Exercise 61

1 My father has lain in bed all day.
2 Each of the girls was at the party.
3 A jar of lollies is on the table.
4 Both mare and foal feed together.
5 Neither of the boys is playing well.
6 Mother has laid the book down somewhere.

Exercise 62

1   The girl was beaten and future games were cancelled.
2   His horse was first and the other two were second and third.
3   The floor has been cleaned and the dishes have been washed.
4   Jones is to be a winger and Smith and Brown are to be forwards.

Exercise 63

1   Illiteracy is the condition of a person who is unable to read or write.
2   Pollution occurs where the environment is spoiled by man-made waste.

Exercise 64

1   The landing at Gallipoli is a special event in Australian history.
2   Banjo Patterson is one of our greatest writers.
3   Robert Menzies ranks as a great prime minister.
4   Captain Cook is responsible for white settlement in Australia.

Exercise 65

1   She decided to walk easily.
2   The team played really well in the first half.
3   My sister plays fairly at cards.
4   Donald is a fair squash player.

Exercise 66

1   The binoculars are handy at the races.
2   His new glasses were on the dining room table.
3   Bring me the pair of knickers that is on the line.
4   A pair of pyjamas was in the bottom drawer.

Exercise 67

1   You will need a saw and a drill.
2   The fisherman uses a rod and reel.
3   This is a gravy and sauce dish.
4   For camping you must take a sleeping bag and a frying pan.

Exercise 68

1 I received with sadness the news of her death.
2 The athletes set a high standard.
3 Someone at school wrote the note.
4 They are building an office on the site.
5 We will appreciate your help. We shall appreciate your help. (better)
6 A contractor is painting the hotel.

Exercise 69

Columbus was a great navigator; he knew the world was round. Colombus was a great navigator. He knew the world was round. Columbus was a great navigator who knew the world was round. Colombus was a great navigator in that he knew the world was round.

Exercise 70

1 The grapes grown in Australia are better than those grown in France.
2 Harold is the stronger of the two brothers.
3 Steven likes Donald better than he likes Michael.
4 Einstein was cleverer than any other man.

Exercise 71

1 The principal wants to see you about the broken window.
2 I was late because the train broke down.
3 Today we should all use calculators.
4 We may yet travel to the stars by nuclear-powered rockets.
5 He should be punished, although he is fifteen.
6 She likes dancing to that kind of music.

Exercise 72

1 His father made a profit when he opened a used-car yard.
2 I understood why Father was so annoyed.
3 The twins were always into mischief after school.
4 The skit is designed to mimic 'Countdown'.
5 I failed at the end of the first year in my course.
6 We had a very enjoyable time at the party.

Exercise 73

1 Bullets or a bomb is not allowed on the plane.
2 One of our men was injured in the crash.
3 Fifty dollars is too much to lose.
4 Jam or butter was not available to the prisoners.

Exercise 74

1　If you want to play tennis well, you must practise.
2　I enjoy swimming because I feel refreshed afterwards.
3　If girls study and they want to become doctors, they can.
4　Some people feel that when they leave school they are entitled to the dole.

Exercise 75

Hiking through the scrub, we were lucky to see the kangaroo. It was sitting quietly, with only its ears moving. Daniel motioned me to keep still while he focused his camera. Suddenly the animal bounded away. This was an example of the shy nature of the kangaroo. (Check with your teacher for any other variations you think are correct.)

Exercise 76

1　He will not come unless I tell him.
2　My brother walks as she does.
3　The man looks like a professional.

Exercise 77

1　NP 2 P 3 NP 4P

Exercise 78

1　For three years running, Brian won the walking race.
2　Looking out of the window of the coach, Mr Smith saw a fox.
3　Mother cooked a meal made of scraps for the visitor.
4　Daniel's hair badly needs cutting.
5　My grandfather is fond of old leather chairs and eating oysters.
6　He telephoned today asking me to come next Sunday.

Exercise 79

1　The visitor, with whom I played golf, was a good player.
2　The woman beside whom I sat was your aunt.
3　Harry, on whose horse I rode, watched me closely.
4　She knew the boy at school from whom she received a letter.
5　My friend, to whom I sent a parcel, received it yesterday.

Exercise 80

1   Have you read that there was an earthquake in Greece?
2   She shared the chips among the three girls.
3   The dog waited beside the front gate.
4   A bus runs past our house.
5   I must have left my purse at home.
6   She is the more aggressive of the two.

Exercise 81

1   We shall be going on holidays next week.
2   I shall be in Israel next month.
3   We will never surrender.
4   She will be travelling by bus in future.
5   He will be at university soon.
6   I will try even harder.

Exercise 82

1   Dianna is one player who may beat me.
2   I cannot bear the thought of his leaving.
3   An argument developed between his sister and him.
4   Do you think it is they who have arrived?
5   Jane is the person who I think spoke to you.
6   We knew we were as strong as they.

Exercise 83

1   She wore a perfect diamond on her finger.
2   His garden is square.
3   This is a very ancient monument.
4   He had a unique Chinese vase on the desk.

Exercise 84

1   Will you let go my dress.
2   Maria asked him whether he was happy.
3   Unless it snows, we cannot ski tomorrow.
4   Apart from Martina, I have not seen a stronger player.
5   Neither Bill nor Dennis can bat well.
6   He drove fast so that he might arrive early.